The Dance Musi

Willie Clancy

Pat Mitchell

Ossian Publications Ltd
Cork, Ireland

THE DANCE MUSIC OF WILLIE CLANCY

ACKNOWLEDGEMENTS

My thanks are due to the following for the advice, information and assistance which they gave me:
My wife Bríd, Terry Moylan, Dr. Seoirse Bodley, Martin Talty, Seán Reid,Seán 'ac Dhonncha, Muiris O Róchāin, Willie's wife Dóirín and especially Breandán Breathnach without whom a work of this nature could not have been conceived, much less executed.
A special word of thanks is due to the council of NA PIOBAIRI UILLEANN for the transfer of goodwill which facilitated the issuing of this new edition of THE DANCE MUSIC OF WILLIE CLANCY
Special thanks are to to Nicholas Carolan for his Discography.

• **Erratum**

continuation of last line on page 11:

. . . musical ability for fluency in Irish. ✓

Photographs of the Willie Clancy School by Liam McNulty N.P.U
Music Origination by Denis Suttill
Illustrations on pages 116 &117 by Wilbert Garvin
Design and Layout by John Loesberg.
Typesetting and continuity by Grace O Halloran

Ossian Publications Ltd
P.O. Box 84, Cork, Ireland.

Printed by Watermans Printers, Cork

ISBN 0 946005 72 9
OMB 39

Contents

Page

OMB 39

In ómós do Bhreandán Breathnach, múinteoir, comhoibritheoir, cara. 1912 - 1985

Chance occurrences can work irrevocable changes on a life. A gift of Breandán's *Ceol Rince 1* gave a first glimpse behind the exciting music I'd fallen in love with.
A chance encounter in Ballinasloe led to an invitation to share in the treasures he had on tape. It introduced a fugitive from Dublin's barren Northside to the glorious music of Johnny McGuire, the Dohertys, Willie Clancy, Seamus Ennis, Dennis Murphy, John Brennan, Junior Crehan and so many more, and led to a long lasting friendship.
Breandán recognised no barriers to achievement - a casual assumption of capability inspired endeavours previously unthinkable. This book is one such.
Tireless to the end in his work of collecting and researching the music he loved, Breandán daily demonstrated that the secret of love is giving, not hoarding - his door was open to all.
For me, his inspiration went far beyond the realms of music; I owe him much.

Preface

To members of Na Píobairi Uilleann the death of Willie Clancy was a grievous blow. The conventional terms of grief and adulation could not serve to express our feelings. We were moved, rather, to record our esteem for Willie as a person and our tremendous indebtedness to him as a musician in some permanent manner. The compilation of a volume of his own music seemed a most fitting way of doing this and so was conceived 'The Dance Music of Willie Clancy'. It is here presented to the numerous musicians who knew him in person or through his music in the hope they find it worthy of the man and the musician we thus commemorate.

The music in this volume has been selected from recordings of Willie's piping held in the society's archive, in other institutes and by private collectors. Pat Mitchell, Secretary of Na Píobairi Uilleann, performed the arduous task of assembling and indexing this material, of adjudicating on the merits of the different tunes available and, then, of transcribing the selected material. He has effected the transcriptions with meticulous accuracy, in many cases in extenso, thus laying before our eyes in all their profusion the forms of ornamentation and variation with which the piper embellishes his music. He has placed us further in his debt by prefixing to this body of music an analysis of the Clancy repertoire and technique of piping. The seal of approval can be accorded to this study since, beside being an accomplished piper himself, he was an intimate friend of Willie Clancy and thus most favourably situated to come to an understanding of his attitude towards the music and its rendition.

Undue modesty should not deter us from drawing attention to some unique features of this work. It is the first collection of Irish pipe music ever to be published; it is the most extensive report on the repertoire of an Irish traditional musician; and the analysis of the music and of the playing techniques presented is the first undertaken in this field.

The inclusion of a conspectus of piping ornamentation and of diagrams illustrating the fingering and range of the chanter, and the tuning of the drones and regulators makes the volume a complete guide to the instrument and its music. By aiding ear and memory it will help the already proficient piper to add with ease to his repertoire. The use of the half moon symbol to indicate the more complex forms of ornamentation, a practice now in general use among music scribes, will permit players other than pipers to use the collection without being distracted with forms of ornamentation not wholly appropriate to their own instruments. And finally, the availability of a body of genuine material presented and commented on authoritatively should prove of interest and value to academic students.

Publication of 'The Dance Music of Willie Clancy' was made possible by the munificence of the Bank of Ireland which most generously agreed to sponsor the work. The local Coiste Cuimhneacháin Willie Clancy (The Willie Clancy Commemorative Committee) expressed a desire to be associated with this commemorative volume and they made a generous contribution towards defraying the expense of publication. The Belfast School of Uilleann Piping drew generously on its funds for this purpose also. A special word of thanks is due to Wilbert Garvin, Council-member of Na Píobairi Uilleann for illustrating the fingering and range of the chanter, and the Tuning of the Drones and Regulators.

OMB 39

Ní fearr bealach ar bith lenár n-ómós do Willie Clancy a fhoilsiú ná cnuasach dá chuid ceoil féin a chur ar fáil don phobal. Thóg Gílbeart, athair Willie, riar mhaith cheoil ó Ghearóid de Barra, píobaire dall a rugadh bliain an drochshaoil, agus d'fhoghlaim Willie an stór seo óna athair.
In áit na seoda fine seo a cheilt ar an slua mar a rinne go leor de na seanphíobairí romhainn roinn Willie go fial flaithúil ar an aos ceoil iad. Níl aon phíobaire a bhuail leis ag Tionól Píobaireachta ná a thug geábh síos go Sráid na Cathrach nach gcasfadh sé dreas ar na píopaí dó i gcruthúnas gur fhága sé oighreacht cheoil nach beag ar théip agus ar chéirnín againn.

Is mór an sásamh do na Píobairí Uilleann cuimhne Willie a bhuanú ar an gcaoi a mb'annsa leis féin, an ceol féin a bhuanú. Is mian liom mo bhuíochas féin agus buíochas an chumainn a ghlachadh le gach duine a chuir ar ár gcumas sin a dhéanamh. Go gcúití Dia a soilíos .

Breandán Breathnach
Cathaoirleach
Na Píobairí Uilleann.
1976

Introduction to the New Edition

December 1972, and a few of us had braved the icy roads to visit Miltown Malbay and Willie Clancy. The high point of the weekend was the session of music after Sunday Mass. Old and unusual tunes were dug out of the recesses of memory and played and delighted over. In the middle of it all, out came - 'Pity, pity we can't roll back the wheel to hear Mickey Cumbaw and Garrett Barry and all of them!' In words as rich as his music, Willie evoked memories of the great pipers whose names had lasted through generations. Words inspired by the conversation, hindsight bestows a ring of prophecy to them; a few short weeks later we too were wishing we could 'turn back the wheel' to meet and hear and be inspired by Willie himself. Universally loved by all those who responded to his openness, his humanity, his sharp-edged - and frequently ribald - wit, his singing, his whistle playing and, of course, his piping, he drew us to his warmth like moths to the flame.

Willie Clancy was a product of the tremendous traditions and love of learning that kept a distinctive culture alive in West Clare. For me Willie was the perfect living example of all that was great hearted and generous in a culture that has now all but disappeared from Ireland. Willie's presence is still so immediate that it is hard to believe twenty years have passed since he died - much less seventeen since this book was published as a memorial to him and his music.

Great changes have occurred in the world of Irish Traditional music during that period. The seventies and early eighties saw the groups become a phenomenon on a par with commercial pop music. People from all over the world with no ethnic Irish connections fell under the spell of the music and began playing it, turning up in their hundreds at the Willie Clancy Summer School and similar events. The mid eighties saw a temporary fall off in the wider popularity of the music paralleled by a growing interest in the set-dancing which had survived mainly in Counties Clare and Kerry. More recently there has been a resurgence of interest - virtuoso performers are captivating audiences with a music in which the lines between Irish Traditional and variously Jazz, Rock, Country and Western, Classical and Cajun, become increasingly blurred. At the same time set-dancing goes from strength to strength and is being taken up enthusiastically not only in Ireland but in Europe, North America and as far away as Australia. And the Céilí band, much despised in recent times, shows signs of making a comeback. So much is happening in the world of Irish Traditional music just now and many influences are being brought to bear on it. In the past, outside influence acted on a well established and relatively conservative body of style and tradition making the music evolve and giving it the vigour we all know and love today. In the process that influence was changed and made into something uniquely Irish. Today mass communication, so life-improving in many ways, is bringing constant and persuasive influence to bear on the Traditional Music. The term 'World Music' is being heard in the middle of discussions about Irish music . . . . If Irish Traditional music is to stay alive and vibrant, it must change but of its very nature it will no longer be traditional if it is overwhelmed by the changes. To guard against this, the music must be approached from a solid base of tradition allowing us shape and control the changes. And what better example of beautiful music steeped in tradition can we find, than in the legacy Willie Clancy left us.

Willie's untimely death in January 1973 removed a key influence from the world of Irish Traditional music. At that time the so-called revival was in full swing and Willie's home town of Miltown Malbay was a western Mecca to which thousands travelled each year. Many of today's well known musicians fell under the spell of the man and his music - at that time, Willie's distinctive ornaments and tunes were to be heard on box, fiddle, flute and pipes alike. Today, these elements are not so immediately apparent. In the intervening years they have been absorbed and adapted to individual styles, leavening and enriching the end results.

Willie himself absorbed influences which reflected his catholic taste in Irish music. To list only one instrument, he spent time listening to and playing music with fiddlers from Sligo, Leitrim, Roscommon, Dublin, Waterford and Kerry. He was an avid student of '78s' sent back from the United States. At one time he fell in love with Ted Fury's banjo playing to the extent that he left Johnny Doran to follow Ted round Dublin. A great singer himself, singing fascinated him, especially the highly ornamented style of Connemara. All of the influences were absorbed and echoes of them could be pinpointed if one cared for such a sterile pursuit. Suffice to say that Willie combined these diverse influences, along with his own artistry, to put an individual stamp on his first love, the music of West Clare. By the time he began playing the pipes Willie was an accomplished performer on whistle and flute. He played a music which had been shaped by the flute, concertina and fiddle playing which surrounded him - the playing of his parents, the Caseys, the Taltys, the Crehans, the Falseys, the Kellys to name but a few. The richness of that music may be sampled on records or, better still, in the playing today of Bobby Casey or Junior Crehan. Remember, too, we hear in the music of Willie Clancy and his compatriots, a strong and vibrant echo of the great Munster Music traditions, the richness of which is otherwise only hinted at in manuscripts and in a meagre handful of Edison cylinder recordings from the turn of the century.

Willie Clancy's legacy to us then, is the music he loved and cherished during his lifetime. A thing of beauty in its own right, having been refined and polished through the generations, Willie's music links us to a part of Ireland's past and makes us, in our turn, bearers of that tradition.

The original edition of The Dance Music of Willie Clancy went through three impressions, being reprinted in 1977 and 1983. Praise is due to John Loesberg and Ossian Publications for their vision in reissuing this tribute to a great man and a great musician. This new edition includes a table of all the triplets played by Willie on various notes. Some typographical errors have been corrected and names have been added to a few 'unknown' tunes. Some interesting photos that came to light have also been included. What has not been included and never can be in transcription - is the excitement, the vitality, the *music* of Willie Clancy. Fortunately, many recordings of his music have now been issued. Find them and listen to them, not, I hasten to add, to learn tunes but for the sheer pleasure of it! These transcriptions would then hopefully become the key to a deeper exploration of Willie's music and some aspects of the West Clare style. And, of course, the dedicated seeker after interesting tunes can be certain the settings are those of a master steeped in tradition. A word of caution here - once a tune is captured in print it can assume undue authority and be taken for the definitive version. These transcriptions show how the tune was played on *one* particular occasion only. Variation is the life blood of Irish Traditional music. In the transcriptions here, Willie Clancy himself shows us just how broad and exciting variation within traditional boundaries can be. Long may his example endure.

Pat Mitchell
An Spidéal

Samhain 1993

Introduction

Much has been written elsewhere about Willie Clancy, the man. For this reason I have made no attempt here at a biography of the great piper. Instead I have tried to set down information given to me by Willie and his friends, about the main events in his life which relate to his music.

Willie was born on Christmas Eve, 1918, in his parents' home just outside Miltown Malbay, in West Clare. His mother, Ellen Killeen, came from an Ennistymon family which was renowned for singing. By all accounts she was a fine singer and Willie got songs from both herself and her sister. She also played the concertina. The Concertina Reel (no. 72) and The Lark in the Morning (no. 78) were said by Willie to be as played by his mother. His father, Gilbert Clancy of Islandbawn, (a district about four miles to the east of Miltown Malbay), also sang and played the concertina; it is as a flute player he is mainly remembered, however. Gilbert Clancy had been a friend of Garrett Barry, the blind piper from Inagh, who died in 1900 but whose memory is very much alive in the locality to the present day, and learned a lot of his music from him. With this background it is not surprising that Willie took to playing the whistle at the age of five. He said once that a neighbour told him at the time 'the whistle is almost as big as yourself!'

The tune Gilbert started him on was 'Father O'Flynn' and it speaks well for Willie's ability that he mastered such a relatively complex tune. Unfortunately I was unable to get hold of a recording of Willie playing this tune on the pipes. The first reel and slip jig that he learned are included, however. These are 'The Ladies' Pantalettes' (no. 82) and 'The First Slip' (no. 30).

As soon as his hands were big enough to span it, he took to playing the flute. Although I never heard him play it myself I have it on good authority that he could do on the flute all the wonderful variations and ornaments we can hear on recordings of his whistle-playing. Eventually he suffered the fate that befell all flute-players - he lost his teeth. When he gave up playing the flute, he passed it on to Martin Talty, the inseparable companion of his youth, who treasures it to this day.

He learned step-dancing from Thady Casey who had danced barefoot to Garrett Barry's playing when a young boy. As well as being a dancing master, Thady played the fiddle and the tambourine, or bodhrán as it is now more commonly known. It was Thady who taught Willie how to play the fiddle. Although he didn't keep in practice, he could certainly knock a tune out of it.

Willie was also a singer in the old style of West Clare, a style which he picked up mainly from his father. It was this intimate knowledge of songs and singing which made his playing of airs on the pipes so much better than that of other musicians, and such a joy to listen to.

Gilbert Clancy's friendship with Garrett Barry made such a lasting impression on him that all through the remainder of his life he spoke glowingly of Garrett's music and personality and automatically compared any music he heard with Garrett's version and performance. Never having heard that Gilbert was a piper but constantly hearing Willie speak of getting Garrett Barry's version of this or that tune from his father, curiosity eventually overcame me and I asked him if his father had played the pipes. 'He played them in his head', said Willie, 'He could never afford to buy a set.'

For much the same reason, Willie, altl
set of pipes in action until he came acros

Willie was immediately fascinated by
that when he first heard Johnny rolling
of tune . This was in 1967 - over thirty y
thinking Johnny Doran could do any w

It was not until 1938 that he managed
Felix. The chanter was a concert pitch c
been made by him as well. As Willie sai

He got some tips from Hugh Curtin of
played many instruments including the
his music from Garrett Barry. Willie also
of Maloney pipes from Hugh which he
Maloney brothers were famous pipe-m
Kilrush who flourished in the 1830's. La
Rowsome in Dublin, but it was Johnny
continually drew him, causing him to fo
place whenever he came within cycling

Willie got his first full set - no less than
Looney, local man in '42 or '43. He nev
working completely to his satisfaction a
Rowsome to make a concert pitch set fo
Coyne set against the price of the new s

By 1947 his piping had improved to s
and won first prize. During the early '40
Potts and Andy Conroy all of whom we

Willie learned the trade of carpentry f
may be seen in the local church. Econo
Dublin in 1951 and later to London in 1
Ennis and absorbed some features of hi

While in Dublin Willie made a habit o
looking for pipes. He continued this pr
which he bought for £5. It was a $17^{1/2}$" s
with keys for F♯, E and D , an octave b

His father died in 1957 and, in the san
the carpentry firm of O'Halloran Bros.

In 1957 he made the recording for Ga
These were made with an $18^{1/2}$" Malone

It was Seán who played the drones on t

Willie Clancy died on January 24th, 1973 and was buried in Ballard cemetery on Friday the 26th. His personality as well as the sense of loss felt by all who knew him was summed up by Seán Mc Kiernan, writing in An Píobaire on the occasion of Willie's death:

"Apart from the permanent sense of loss which is overwhelming, we suffer the loss of more than just an artist. For me Willie represented the old way of life (a thing I value beyond words) and this *'Bealach an tsean-nóis'* came through so strongly, not only in his piping, whistling or singing, but in conversation with him, in his hospitality even, and in this day and age when what he stood for tends to become so watered down and artificialised through bright lights, his loss is so much greater . . . . From the beginning no other music could interest or satisfy me as fully as Willie's, and now he is dead we starve."

Willie Clancy (1960's) Picture courtesy of Gerry Hillary, Miltown Malbay

The Tunes

The 152 tunes in this book represent all of Willie Clancy's tunes, excluding airs, that I managed to gather together up to Christmas 1975. My original intention was to transcribe the airs as well but this proved to be such a formidable task that I was forced to abandon it. They will be published separately, it is hoped, at a later date.

I should say, at the outset, that the transcriptions in this collection are not to be regarded as the definitive versions of the tunes. Although all of Willie's versions were good it would be wrong to regard them as the only correct ones. A glance at any of the tunes which I have transcribed at length will show that Willie himself did not think there was only one correct way to play a tune; he kept changing it as he went along. To illustrate the point I have included two transcriptions of the same basic version of 'Garrett Barry's Jig' (nos 36 and 59) as played on different occasions. Of a total of 18 bars (including change on repeats) only bars 5, 7 and 12 are played identically, even bars which have identical notes such as 3 and 10 being played staccato on one occasion and legato on the other.

My modus operandi was to transcribe the first playing of the tune, including repeats if the variations warranted this. In many instances, however, the tune was transcribed from one only known recording. As most of these recordings were made by enthusiasts at music sessions it happened quite frequently that the first few bars were missed. What I did in such cases was to use the second or third playing of the tune. On some occasions, due to a defect in the playing or the recording, this was not possible and here it was necessary to patch together the last few bars of the first playing and the first few bars of the repeat to achieve a complete part. That so much of what was casually put on tape was faultless is a testimony to the excellence of Willie's playing.

The availability of only one recording led to my having to include a number of odd-sounding bars in the transcriptions, e.g. bar 4 of 'Give Us a Drink of Water' (no. 123). The first seven bars were completely missing, thus necessitating the use of the second playing of the tune. As it stands bar 4 is perfectly acceptable as a variation in a repeat but normally bars 4 and 8 would be identical on a first playing. Another example is the second version of 'The Dublin Reel' (no. 52). Having played the normal version Willie went on to show me how it could be played in 'C', playing it over only once and finishing it with a fine flourish. A whole new ending would have to be reconstructed to make this version playable in the normal way. Bars 19 and 20 (the 3rd and 4th bars of the last part) or a variation of them should be adequate. (See Breandán Breathnach's *Folk Music and Dances of Ireland*, chapter 2, on the structure of dance music.).

Although this book is about the *dance* music of Willie Clancy I have included some items which do not fit into this category. Two of these, 'The Humours of Glin' (no. 54) and Nóra Críona (no. 150) are what is known in piping as 'pieces'. The piece is a jig which has been slowed down and highly ornamented and it is possible that the professional pipers of the past were expected to be capable of playing many jigs in this fashion.

Willie learned these pieces from local musicians. He had no jig version of 'The Humours of Glin' and, in the case of 'Nóra Críona' he got the piece and the basic version of the jig (no. 151) from different sources. I have also included (no. 152) the version of the jig he usually played and which he called 'Patsy Tuohey's Version.'

Another two slow items are 'The Trip We Took Over The Mountains' (no. 128), a song air, and 'The Old Man Rocking the Cradle' (no. 130) which is related to the song 'An Seanduine.'

Both of these tunes give the impression of having quite a marked rhythm. When I came to transcribe them, however, I discovered, that to achieve the effect he wanted, Willie had lengthened some notes and shortened others to the extent that the end result was practically in free rhythm. I decided to treat them in a fashion suggested to me by remarks made by Dr Seoirse Bodley on the notation of *sean-nós* singing, viz. that all *sean-nós* songs have a basic underlying rhythm and can be written as such with the divergences indicated. I therefore wrote the song in strict rhythm, showing by pauses of various lengths the notes on which Willie dwelt.

The names of the tunes are those I heard being used by Willie. I could not discover any name for a few of the tunes and these I have left anonymous.

The order in which the tunes appear represents a kind of personal chronology.
The transcriptions begin with tunes from two Gael-Linn 78 rpm recordings which I bought before I had commenced playing the pipes and which were partly the cause of my being attracted to this instrument. They end with some tunes which I recorded for Na Píobairí Uilleann when, with members of that group, we paid Willie Clancy a visit. That visit ended on 10 December 1972, only a few weeks before his death.

Generally speaking, the groups of tunes appear in the order in which I came across them (the groups are noted in the acknowledgements), the only exception being those recent acquisitions from people who responded to my appeal for material. These I have inserted immediately prior to the December 1972 group.

With the exception of 'The Mountain Road' (no. 38) and 'The Shaskeen' (no. 110) both of which Willie got from fiddlers and left largely unaltered, the tunes as transcribed could be classed as piping versions. This does not mean that they are suitable only for playing on pipes. They are quite suitable for whistle, flute, fiddle or accordion.

I should like to say a special word about this collection to those who might use it as an aid to learning Irish music. Irish music is part of an oral/aural tradition and it is impossible to convey the nuances of phrasing, rhythm and tone on paper. So I would urge those people to seek out Willie's recordings and learn their music from them, using this book only as a guide to the notes played by him.

'Willie had a great love for Children'.
Photo by Terry Wilson, Miltown Malbay and 'Raftery's Rest', Kilcolgan, Galway.

Signs, Terms and Ornaments

To keep the transcription as legible as possible I have used the half-circle sign to indicate the ornaments known as rolls and crans (see page 23). This sign was originally devised by Breandán Breathnach for Ceol Rince na hÉireann and is now widely used in the notation of Irish music. In these tables I have given the most widely accepted written versions of the ornaments but it should be borne in mind that crans and rolls although introduced to vary the melody are essentially rhythmic devices and depend for their effect on being played with the correct rhythm rather than with any melodically correct set of notes. The actual notes played can, and do, vary from player to player; they can also vary in the playing of a single tune. It depends on the direction from which the rolled note is approached, the fingering in use immediately before and after the note, or the special effect desired. Take the roll on F for example. It may be played in the basic fashion (ex. A) or without lifting the E fingers (ex. B). The rhythm of the roll still comes through perfectly when played like this. Or it may be played to get a strong accent combined with a very striking tonal effect (ex. C). Once again the E fingers are not lifted but the chanter is raised off the knee just as the first grace note of the roll is sounded. This last method is in fact the way in which the F♯ rolls in 'The Dublin Reel' (no. 51) were treated. Some further aspects of Willie's rolling and cranning are dealt with later.

Rolls are sometimes shown as example D and some musicians - Patsy Tuohey for one - played them in this way. The more popular way and the way in which Willie played them is to make the lower or final grace note (in ex. D it would be the F♯ in the triplet) of shorter duration than the first one. In practice this is achieved by merely flicking the finger at the vent in question rather than making a positive closure.

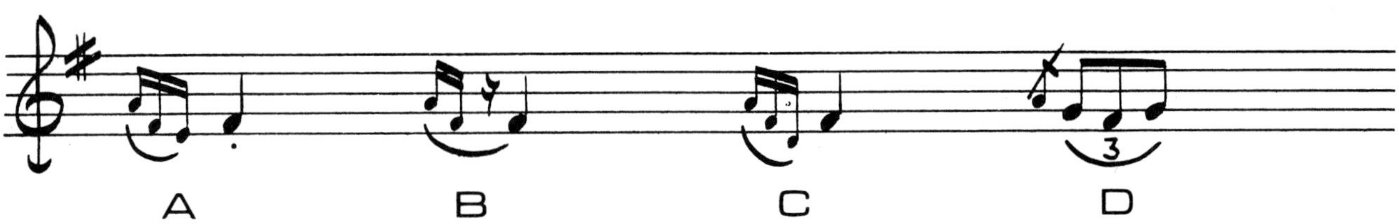

The grace notes in the cran are of shorter duration than the first grace note in the roll. The cranning effect is achieved by sounding each grace note individually with a very positive finger action; the note being cranned is audible between each grace note.

The sign ↗ is used to indicate a slide up to the note at which it is pointed. In most cases a short slide is intended from slightly below the note in question up to full pitch. In the case of a 'C', however, the slide is often quite protracted and the note sustained with slight flattening of the pitch.

The sign 𝄐 is used to designate a pause of from two to four times the indicated length of the note. ⌈•⌉ designates a pause of from four to six times the indicated length. ⌈⌈•⌉⌉ designates a pause of greater than six times the indicated length. A comma (,) placed over the stave indicates a momentary closure of the chanter. These signs are used only in nos 128 and 130.

I have made use of two other devices to convey more information than they would in conventional notation. The first is the staccato sign when it appears over the note 'C'. In all instances this indicates a staccato C♯ was played irrespective of the key signature of the tune in question. On the pipes it is possible to get away with this, due in part to a certain vagueness of pitch about C♯ and C♮ to begin with, and in part to the very short duration of the note. The m ain reason for using C♯ is to avoid the loss of attack that would result from the use of a staccato C♮, the sounding of which would necessitate the raising of three fingers together. On instruments other than pipes the accented staccato 'C' would be played in the pitch indicated by the key signature.

The other device I have used unconventionally is the grace note E' leading on to D' (the thumb note). This, in fact, is a piping device known as 'the ghost D'. It is actually pitched about D' sharp and is produced by raising only the little finger of the lower hand. It has none of the cutting effect of the usual grace note, being played very legato, but it gives a strange tonal quality to the thumb note when heard over the drones.

Tipping, a term used to describe a type of variation in which repeated staccato notes are used (exx. E and F), is somewhat misleading in that the finger action used to produce the effect is the very opposite to that of tipping, it being required to place the chanter on the knee and hold it closed while each note is released consecutively. If the note is held open and the chanter 'tipped' with the finger the typical tipping sound is not produced. Examples E and F below used as variations will be found in bars 29 and 30 of 'Coppers and Brass' (no. 41). An excellent example of Willie's use of tipping as a variation may be found in bar 17 of the repeat of 'Nellie Donovan' (no. 19).

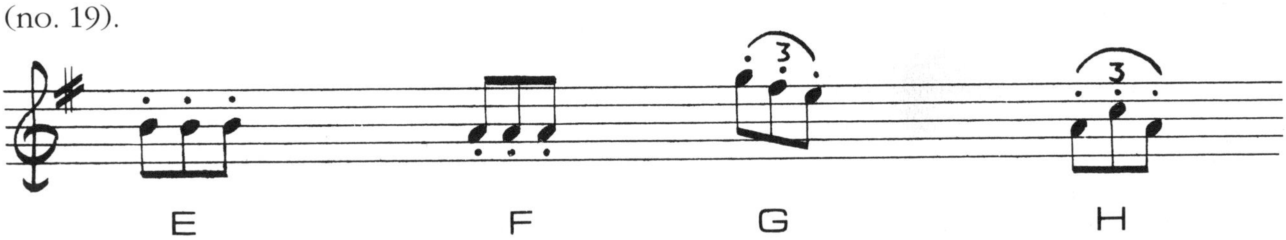

Besides conforming with conventional musical usage the triplet as a form of ornamentation in piping is employed ad lib., quite frequently with staccato (tight) fingering. An apt description of this type of fingering is contained in the admonition by Leo Rowsome 'that the staccato notes must snap out like pistol shots'. The fingering required to produce the tight triplet is identical with that described for tipping.

The triplet most used by Willie was the tight triplet of G' F'♯ E' (ex. G.). This occurs in no less than 70 tunes in the collection. Next in popularity is the tight triplet A C♯ A (ex. H.). No other triplets occurred nearly so frequently but the examples at I (in both octaves) J, K and L (in descending order of usage) were also widely used. Willie also made frequent use of legato (open) triplets, the most-used one being E' F♯ ' G'. (ex M). Other open triplets favoured by Willie are examples N and O (in both octaves) and examples P, Q and R, (in descending order of usage).

In the ornamental tight triplet, the main accent, on the first note, is produced by making it very staccato; a secondary accent is created on the last note, by lengthening it slightly. This holds true whether this form of ornamentation appears in common time or triple time tunes. In some jigs, however, instead of simply making a triplet out of two of the quavers Willie played four notes of more or less equal weight turning the normal jig triplet into a quadruplet. An example of the same note sequence used in both these forms will be found in 'Sixpenny Money' (no. 18).

Finally 'popping' is the name given to the act of momentarily lifting the chanter off the knee to accentuate a note by increasing its volume. If performed very quickly a sound akin to a dog's bark is produced.

Liam Og O Floinn and Willie Clancy
(Mal Whyte Photos, Loaned by NPU)

The Music

Before embarking on a detailed investigation of aspects of Willie's playing, some consideration of piping style in general is necessary. There are two main schools of piping. 'Tight' and 'open' might best describe the difference between them. Basically one can say tight piping is achieved by opening only those vents on the chanter necessary to sound the required note and open piping by closing only those vents necessary to sound the note.
This is to oversimplify matters somewhat although there have been, and are, people who follow the two extremes, i.e. those who play completely open, others who play so tight (with noticeable stops between each note) that their playing has a completely staccato sound.

Willie Clancy's style was a highly personal one and, taken overall, would lie between the two main schools of piping. Some of his fingering and some of his tunes were very much influenced by Johnny Doran's open style, e.g. 'The Star of Munster' (no. 64), while other parts of his playing show signs of the later influence of John Potts and Séamus Ennis and various recordings of tight piping which he heard, amongst them those of Patsy Touhey, Mike Gallagher and Mike Carney. In fact the first tune in the book derives from the playing of Mike Gallagher whose piping was staccato throughout.

One of the most notable features of Willie's playing was the constant variation and I have transcribed a number of tunes at length to illustrate this point. It should be noted that much of the variation is effected, not by changing the melody but by changing the ornamentation. A good example of this will be found in 'Old Tipperary' (no. 17) where, in the basic form, bars 2, 6, 10 and 14 would be identical. However, we find that in bar 2 staccato tipping on 'A' and a long roll on 'G' were employed, in bar 6, staccato quadruplet on A and a long roll on G, in bar 10 staccato tipping on A and G and in bar 14 long rolls on both A and G. Note also the matching up of the slide on C in bar 3 with the open rolling on G in bar 2 and the staccato C in bar 11 with the tipping on G in bar 10.

In single-line music such as we are dealing with here such variation is all-important, more especially now that its audience is changing from dancer to the listener, although the piper appears always to have had a following which preferred to listen rather than dance to his music. The need for variation becomes obvious if the scale of existence of the tunes is considered. Take the reel for example: the majority of reels consisted of two parts of eight bars each.
The usual practice is to play each part twice, then repeat the performance. Even taken at a reasonably steady pace, this will take no longer than about seventy seconds or a little over a second per bar. So, when the first bar of the first part is repeated, only eight seconds have elapsed since the first playing - too short an interval in which to forget what has been previously played. Taking the argument a further step, when the whole tune comes to be repeated only thirty-two seconds will have elapsed since the previous playing of any bar - once again, quite a short interval.

An even greater need for variation occurs in those reels which consist of two four bar phrases, each phrase being repeated to make up the eight bars of the full part. Each eight-bar part is played over once only or 'singled' as it is called. An excellent example of the way in which Willie went about handling one of these tunes is 'Nellie Donovan' (no. 19). Looking down along the tune it immediately becomes obvious that the only bar which is consistently repeated is the concluding one of each part. This repeat of a concluding bar without change is an aspect of Willie's playing which may be noted in many of the tunes.

If we take the first four bars as Willie's basic version of the part we see on the repeat of the first bar that although the same notes are used the rhythm has changed to put the accent on the C rather than the A of the first playing. Likewise a change of rhythm in the second bar shifts the accent from the second crotchet G to the first crotchet B and changes the second crotchet to two quavers G and B. They, in turn, give a lead-in to the second group which has now become four separate quavers. The arrangement of the notes in this group viz. going two down and one up is a very strong rhythmic device much used by Willie. (See also bars 4, 8, 12, 16 of 'The Dublin Reel', no. 51). Once again we get a shift in rhythm in the first group of notes of the next bar, the accented B not only appears later in the bar but is ornamented by a short roll. This is led up to by G and B which gives a lot more *body* to the sound produced by that group of notes. We now come to the first variation proper. Here Willie makes use of the Johnny Doran device of repeating notes and compressing the range of the melody for effect, by dropping the C of bar 3 above to B and separating it from the rolled B with yet another grace note. This gives a very smooth effect in which B can be heard right through, overlaid by all the grace notes. The movement is finished off nicely by raising the second A by a fifth to E, thus giving a great 'lift' to the music before the part is concluded in the next bar.

Once again the first four bars of the second part can be taken as his basic version. In bar 5, the repeat of the first bar, we see him using the G' F♯' E' not merely to change from the E' crotchet of the first playing but to give a sense of conclusion which is completed by the jumps to B' and A' in the second last bar. This last device is commonly used in the playing of reels.

Coming to the repeat of the first part we find that he has used tipping on the B and the A to make a very striking variation of the first bar, the second bar is similar to the first playing, and the tipped first bar is reflected in the use of a staccato B plus roll in the third bar.

The second four bars of the repeat are similar to the original four with the exception of the Doran touch on the first note of the second bar, where the B has been brought down to A giving an effect similar to that on the B in the seventh bar of the tune. This repetition, almost, of the first playing shows great economy in the use of variation. We have had this 4 bar section changed extensively since first hearing it and as the ear will tend to compare it with the more recent repeat(s) this return to basic form will now itself sound like a variation.

Participants (Fiddle) at the Willie Clancy Summer School
(Photo: Liam McNulty)

The repeat of the second part was similar to its first playing. A feature that may be noted among musicians who vary their music as they go along is this variation of one part with little or no variation of another until perhaps the third or fourth repeat.

It is necessary, in considering these points, that the highly compressed form of Irish music be kept in mind. I know only too well that it can be quite meaningless to the person who is not used to listening to this finer detail - when I first heard Irish music it took about a year for me to be able to distinguish between tunes and many more years of repeated listening to the same material before I could hear and appreciate everything that was being done in it .

In going through the tune above I made a number of references to 'accents'. In that tune the accents referred to were fairly obvious in that they fell on crotchets or dotted crotchets in a tune which is built predominantly on quavers. Basically speaking the chanter has a fixed volume output and in a group of, say, four quavers, the accented notes are brought out by dwelling on them a little longer than on the unaccented notes. Another device used is to 'pop' the chanter while dwelling on the note thus getting a very strong accent. The note may also be accentuated by 'cutting' it with a grace note. An example of the combination of the three devices, although the chanter is not in fact popped but held off the knee for about a bar and a half, may be found in the second part of 'The Bucks of Oranmore' (no. 32). In bar 13 the chanter is raised to make the bottom D and cran. Willie then held it off the knee, used a grace note to 'cut' the A which was sounded by lifting the A finger only. Replacing that finger automatically sounded bottom D. The B in that bar and the A in the following one were played in the same way, the chanter being replaced on the knee for B in bar 14. The intervening D's being so short and effectively muted by blending in with the drones, the sequence of notes A B A appears to drift out of the music in a somewhat disembodied fashion. This occurs without the loss of rhythm that would result from playing a crotchet each on A, B and A which, subjectively, the effect resembles.

A distinctive feature of Willie's playing was the many ways in which he accented the note 'C'. I have already mentioned the staccato C, noting that it is always played as C♯. The staccato C is sounded for a very short duration - a little longer than a grace note and the accent is brought out by making the stop after it long enough so that, taken together, note and stop take up the same time as would dwelling on the C to accent it. The finger action Willie used to sound this note - keeping the finger straight and snapping it off the chanter- is in direct contrast to the way in which he fingered the C♮. For this note he simply uncurled his finger from the chanter keeping the lower part of the second joint in contact with it. At all times the finger was in contact with the edge of the C vent. The effect of doing this is to flatten the pitch slightly and, more importantly, to give a very individual tone to the note. It also facilitated the making of a slide, in that the finger only had to be uncurled slowly to do this. Examples of the use of staccato and slide on an accented C will be found in bars 1 and 3 respectively of 'Old Tipperary' (no.17). In bars 1 and 4 respectively of 'Strop the Razor' (no. 29) the same devices will be found with, in addition, grace notes to further accentuate them. The position in which these grace notes appear are peculiar to Willie's playing. When going from D' to C he would momentarily close the chanter then sound the D' grace note before playing 'C'. It is perhaps more obvious in bar 24 of 'Colonel Frazer' (no. 87) where the D' is played full staccato readily enabling the grace note to be sounded.

Willie made use of the slide as an ornament to add interest to a note which was already accented by virtue of its length. An example of this may be seen in bar18 (2nd bar of 2nd part) of 'The Old Bush' (no. 3). The slide in this case was quite protracted and to add to the interest of the note a strong vibrato was used as well.

At the Tionól Piobaireachta at Bettystown, Co Meath in 1969, playing a left-handed set of Moss Kennedy Pipes, made specially for Sean McKiernan.

One other method of playing C was employed by Willie. When going from E' to C he very often made the C by leaving the E fingers open and lifting the C finger. This produces a note which is about midway in pitch between the C♯ and the C♮ on the pipes. Its most notable feature, however, is the distinctive tone it produces and this is the reason he used it. The C in bars 8, 13, 15 and 21 of 'Corney is Coming' (no. 8) were all made in this way.

Willie frequently used grace notes to introduce accents to the off beats when playing jigs. Examples of grace notes used on and off the beat will be found in one of his versions of 'The Frieze Breeches' (no. 12). In bar 2 the D' grace note is used to accentuate the beat on C. In bar 3 the grace note B accentuates A, the middle note of the triplet which would usually carry the least accent. In bar 39 (the second last bar in the tune) the second triplet is graced both on and off the beat, the accent on the off beat giving a wonderful lifting or skipping effect before the tune is concluded.

Another way in which Willie achieved this skipping effect on the off beat was by raising it a number of tones. In 'The Galbally Farmer' (no. 141), in bar 7, he plays the triplet C A F♯ leading to the G in bar 8 in the normal fashion. When he comes to play the same triplet in bar 15 however he raises the last note by a sixth, playing C A D' to lead on to the G in bar 17.

Willie's roll-playing deserves special attention. In 'The Ravelled Hank of Yarn' (no. 2) may be seen examples of the way in which both the long and the short roll are usually introduced to tunes. In bar 1 the long roll is used to ornament the first three of each group of four quavers. In bar 2 the short roll is used to ornament the second two of each group of four quavers, the roll being played on a crotchet of the same pitch as the preceding quaver. This is the way in which the short roll is most often used. Moving on to bars 14 and 15, which in their basic form would be similar, we find the short roll used as a variation on the long one. Although appearing in the same second crotchet position of the other short rolls, its effect is very different because it is preceded by a staccato crotchet.

In bar 5 of 'The Old Bush' (no. 3) there is an example of a short roll played on a crotchet of a different pitch from the preceding note. There is a practical consideration here, in that Willie invariably used the A grace note when playing the G roll and if the music were played exactly as shown there would be no way in which a grace note could be accommodated.

Willie had two ways of meeting this difficulty. In the example quoted and in all other tunes similarly notated, what Willie did, was momentarily to close the chanter after the A then re-open it to make the A grace note. In reality it would appear as example S. His other solution to the problem was to hit the lower note, immediately gracing it with the A as in bar 17 of 'The Fermoy Lasses' (no. 16). Written fully it would become as example T.

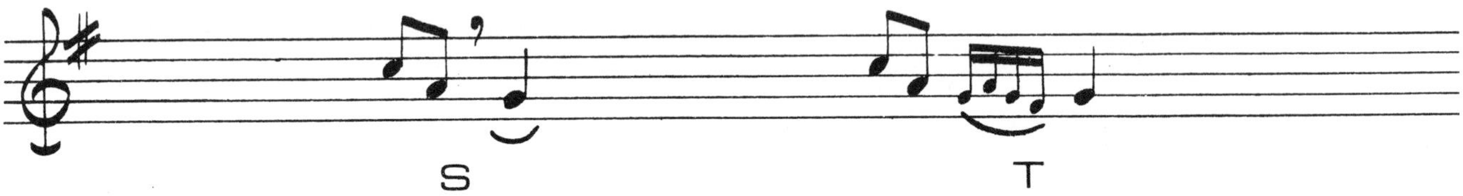

The G roll in bar 17 of 'The Fermoy Lasses' offers an example of the way in which Willie used the short roll to start the bar. Perhaps his most novel use of the short roll was in his 'double' or, more correctly, multiple rolling. Examples of this occurring on various notes will be found will be found in bar 18 of 'Bean Tincéara' (no. 6), bar 33 of 'The Bucks of Oranmore' (no. 32) and bars 5 and 31 of 'Tarbolton' (no. 14). Willie also doubled long rolls and crans and an example of the rolls will be found in bar 14 of 'The Humours of Derrykissane' (no. 22), of crans on E, in bars 2 and 3 of 'Willie's Single' (no 75) and on D in bar 17 of 'Pis Fhliuch' (no 39).

Finally he sometimes used a double roll which combined both long and short roll mainly in the last bar of a part. An example is bar 9 of 'The Pipe on the Hob' (no. 5). Willie frequently played a variant of the long roll on the notes F♯ and B. This variant makes uses of the short roll rhythm on the second two of the group of four quavers in the reel or three in the jig. The first quaver, however, is played a note lower than the note being rolled and gives a great feeling of '*body*' to the roll. A somewhat similar effect is achieved where he drops the F♯ preceding a normal F♯ roll to bottom D as in bar 6 of 'The West Wind' (no. 33). This device, which was probably derived from Johnny Doran's playing, combined with a variant of Patsy Touhey's double-cut-type G roll is used with great effect in bars 18 and 19 of 'Strop the Razor' (no. 29). The use of the grace note to introduce the long roll on G and then the repeat of that roll followed by the F♯ roll variant is unique to Willie's playing.

Crans and Rolls

The back 'D' (or thumb note) is not rolled or cranned. For the convenience of other musicians, the forms appropriate to other instruments are reproduced at page 124

1. Played with the chanter **off** the knee and little finger down
2. Played with the chanter **on** the knee and little finger raised

Tables of Triplets and Quadruplets used by Willie Clancy in the Transcribed Tunes

'D'

'E'

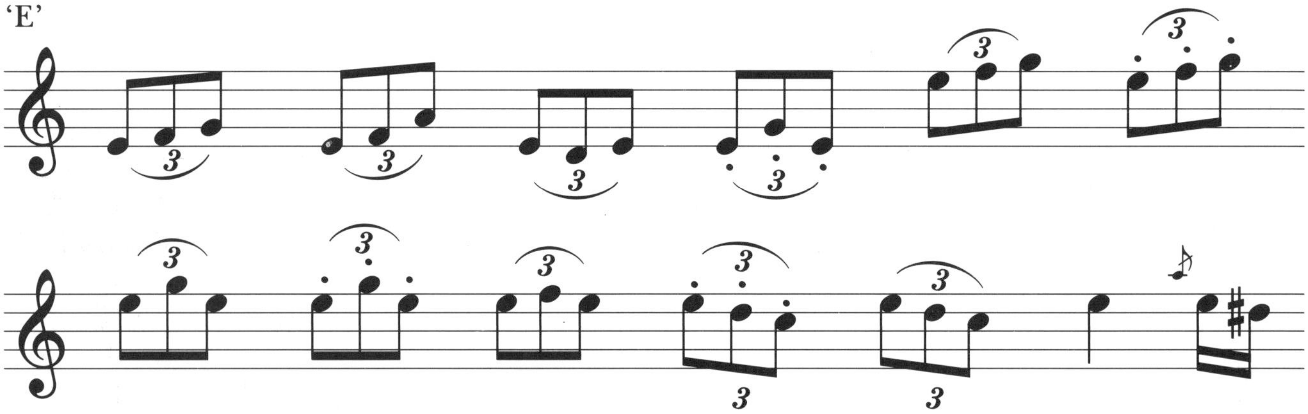

'F'

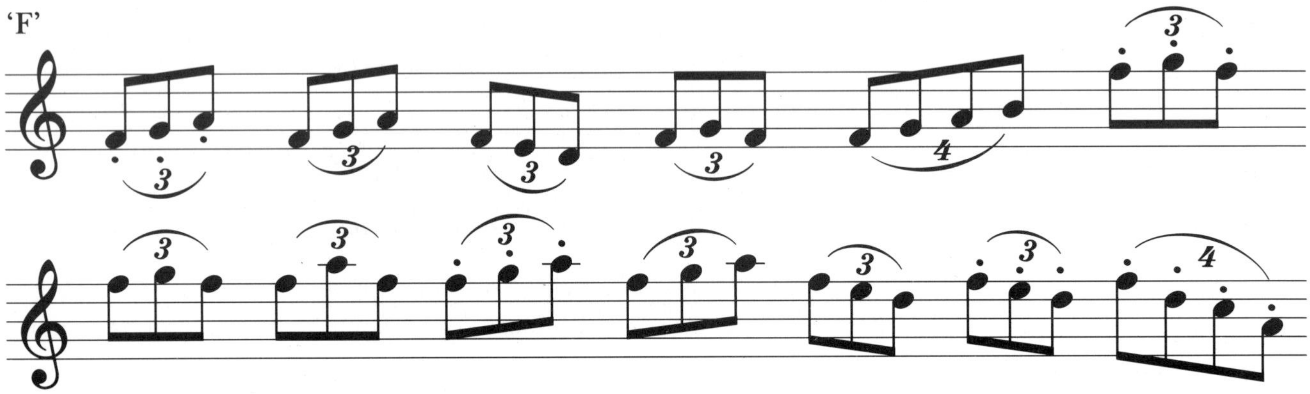

'G'

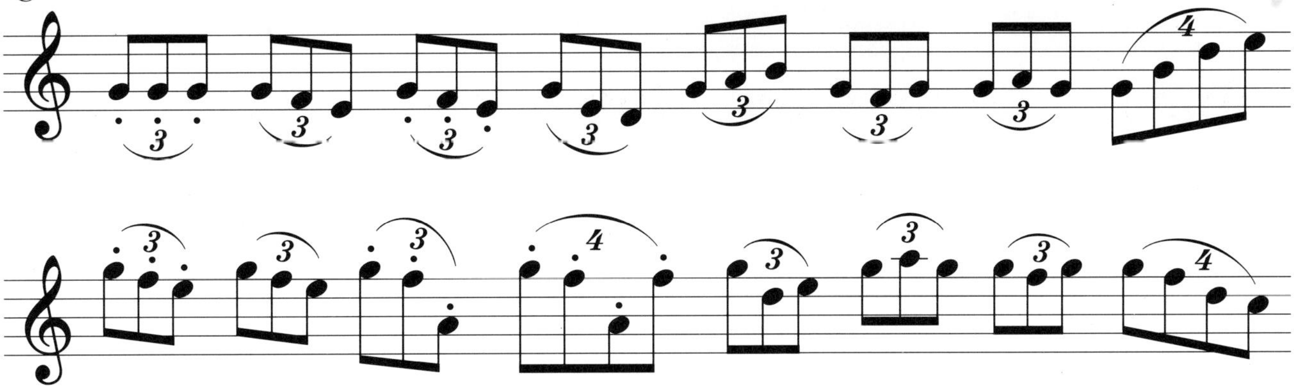

'A'

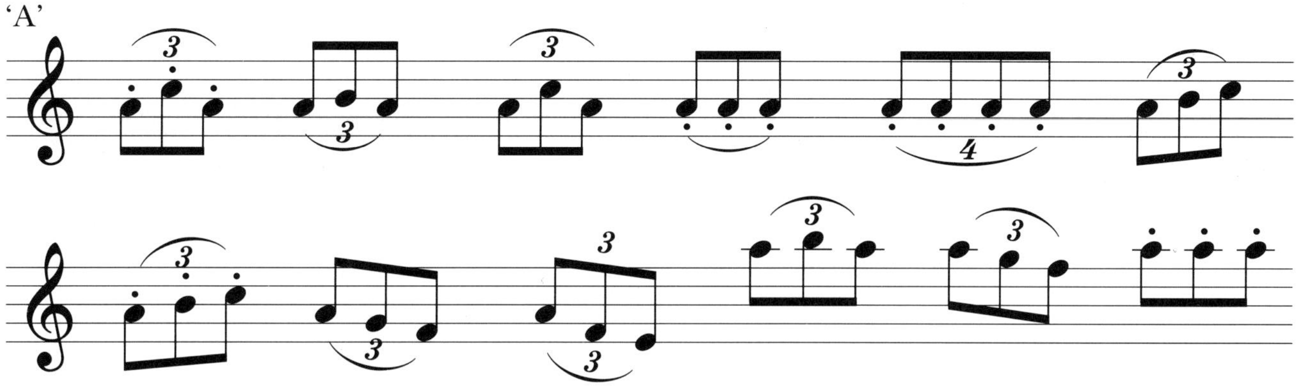

'B'

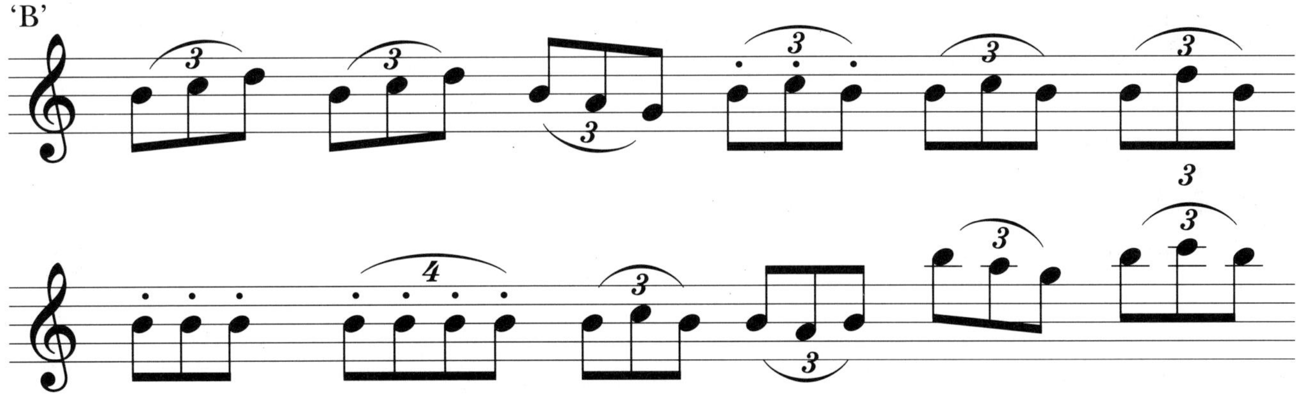

'C'

Tabulated above are all the triplets, quadruplets and related ornaments used by Willie Clancy in the tunes transcribed. A number of them are dealt with in detail in the introduction. 'Tight' versions of the ornaments are shown in the convention used throughout thhe original transcriptions, that is, with staccato marks on each note. While Willie Clancy did tend to use strongly staccato fingering, more recent research would indicate the 'tight' effect can be achieved without making each note staccato. (See 'The Piping of Patsy Touhey').

Johnny Doran (right) and friends, circa 1946
(Photo: NPU)

Willie Clancy and Gaelic League Branch members at Celtic Congress in Quimper, Brittany, July 1951. (Photos by courtesy of Harry Hughes)

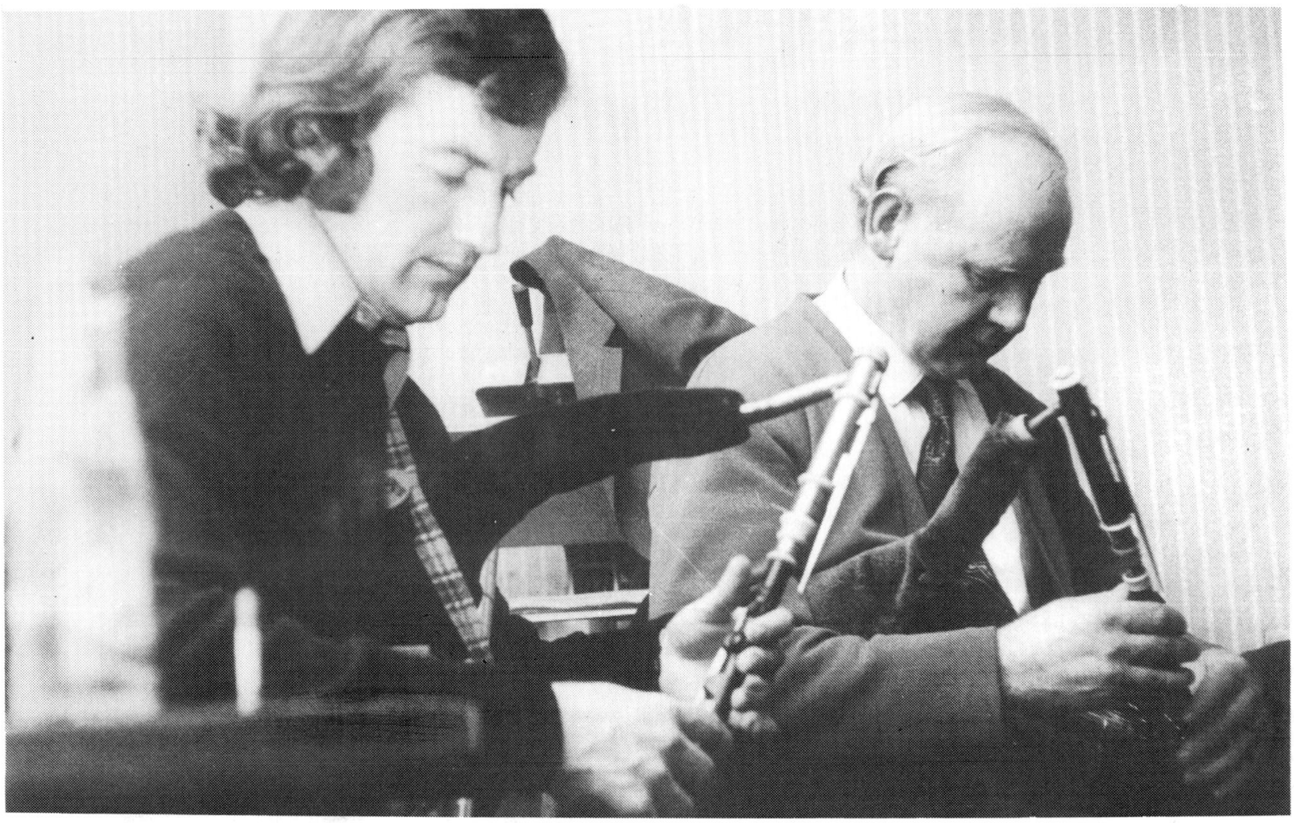

With Liam Og O Floinn
(Mal Whyte Photos, loaned by NPU)

1 The Plains of Boyle

2 The Ravelled Hank of Yarn

3 The Old Bush

4 The Leitrim Fancy

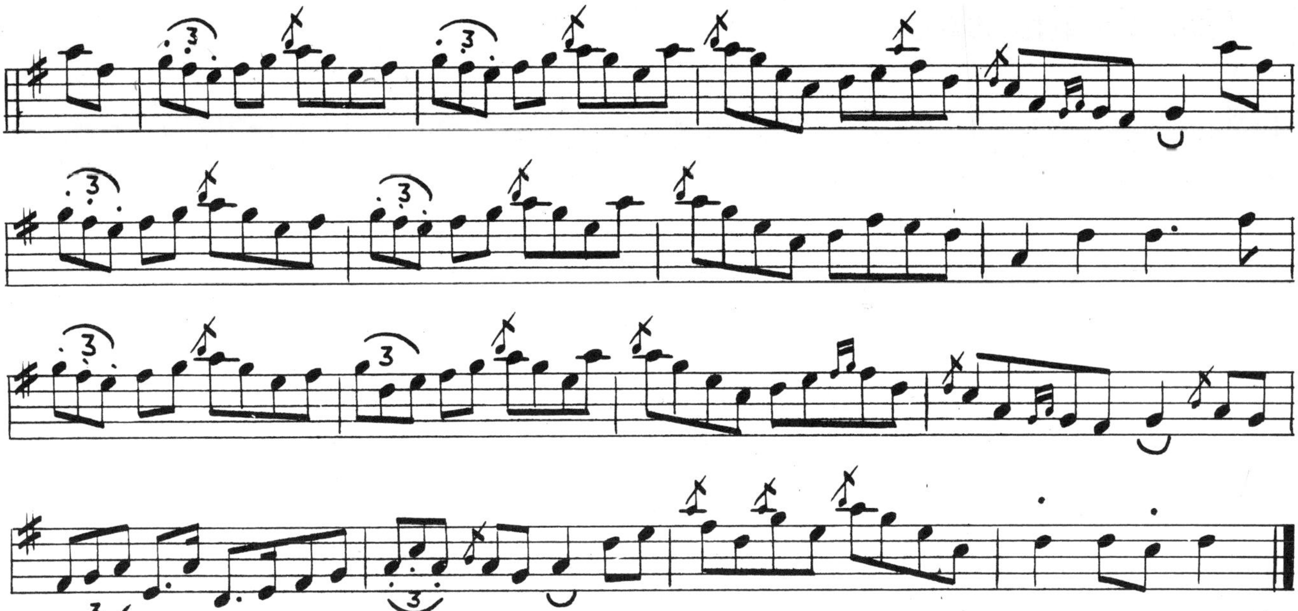

5 The Pipe on the Hob

OMB 39

6 An Bhean Tincéara

7 Bímid ag Ol

8 Corney is Coming

9 The Concert Reel

10 The Fisherman's Lilt

11 The Frieze Breeches

12 The Frieze Breeches

13 Lucy Campbell

14 Tarbolton

15 Seán Reid's Reel

16 The Fermoy Lasses

17 Old Tipperary

18 Sixpenny Money

19 Nellie Donovan

20 Jenny Tie Your Bonnet

21 Tiocfaidh Tú Abhaile Liom

OMB 39

22 The Humours of Derrykissane

23 Garrett Barry's Reel

24 The Virginia

25 The Boy on the Hilltop

26 Máirseáil Alasdruim

27 Farewell to Erin

28 The Lady's Bonnet

29 Strop the Razor

30 The First Slip

31 Kitty's Gone a-Milking

OMB 39

32 The Bucks of Oranmore

33 The West Wind

34 Scatter the Mud

35 Seán Buí

36 Garrett Barry's Jig

37 The Collier's Reel

38 The Mountain Road

39 An Phis Fhliuch

OMB 39

40 The Clare Jig

41 Coppers and Brass

42 The Rolling Wave

43 Sruthán a' Chait

44 The Harvest Home

45 The Mountain Lark

OMB 39

46 Will You Come Down to Limerick?

47 The Boy in the Gap

48 The Braes of Busby

49 'Chailleach, do Mhairís Mé

50 Ceol na gCeártan

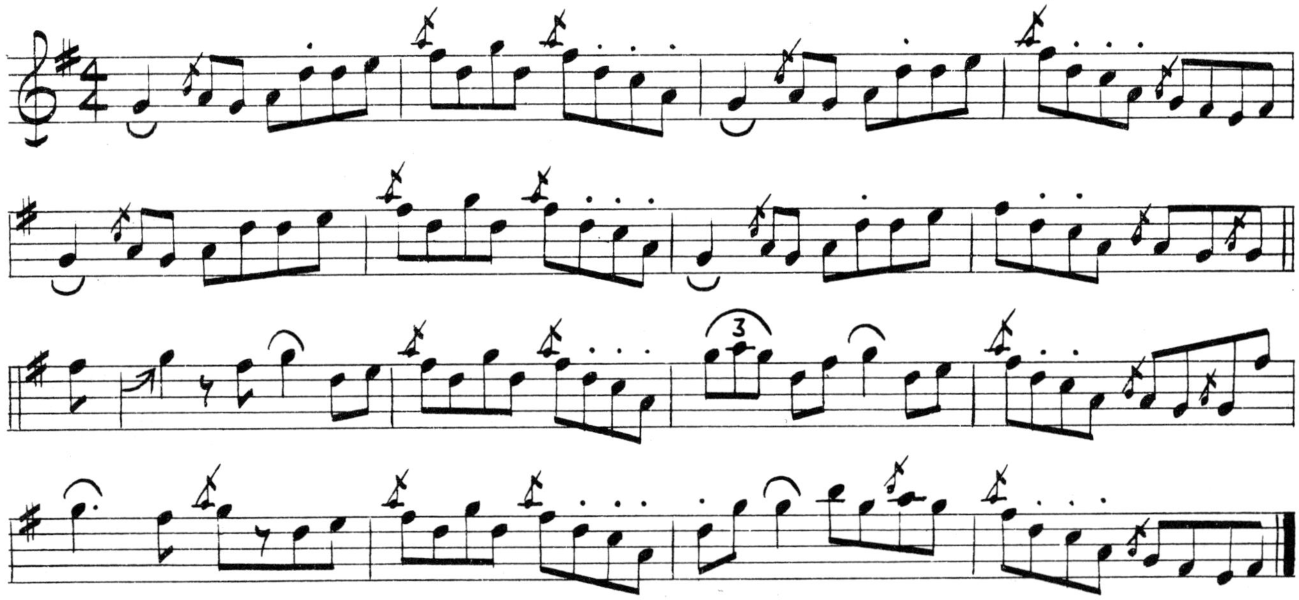

51 The Dublin Reel

52 The Dublin Reel

OMB 39

53 The Boys of Ballisodare

54 The Humours of Glin

55 The Milliner's Daughter

OMB 39

56 The Old 'Wheels of the World'

57 Unknown

58 Will You Come Down to Limerick?

OMB 39

59 Garrett Barry's Jig

60 Páidín O Raifearta

61 Páidín O Raifearta

62 The Connacht Heifers

63 Rakish Paddy

64 The Star of Munster

to finish

65 The Copperplate

66 The Maiden that Jigs it in Style

67 The Dublin Lads

68 Unknown

69 The Mayo Lasses

70 Unknown

71 The Green Groves of Erin

72 The Concertina Reel

73 Fasten the Leg in Her

74 The Fowler on the Moor

75 Willie's Single

76 Petticoat Loose

77 Down the Broom

78 The Lark in the Morning

79 The Ballintore Fancy

80 The Langstern Pony

OMB 39

81 The Crooked Road to Dublin

82 The Ladies' Pantalettes

83 My Love is in America

84 The Hunt

85 Garraí na Saileog

86 Fraher's Jig

87 Colonel Frazer

88 The Flowers of Edinburgh

89 Seán O Duibhir an Ghleanna

90 The Campbells are Coming

91 Merrily Dance the Quaker

92 I'll Mend Your Pots and Kettles O

OMB 39

93 The Maid of Montcisco

94 Cherish the Ladies

95 Green Fields of America

96 The Ivy Leaf

97 The Groves Hornpipe

98 Kelly's Hornpipe

99 Poll Halpenny

100 The Yellow Tinker

101 The Frieze Breeches

102 The Frieze Breeches

103 Down the Back Lane

104 Unknown

105 The Cook in the Kitchen

106 The Ewe Reel

107 The Cup of Tea

108 The Sweep's Hornpipe

109 The Killimer Jig

110 The Shaskeen

111 The Lark in the Morning

112 The Lark in the Morning

113 The Banks of Lough Gowna

114 The Friendly Visit

115 The First of May

116 The Curragh Races

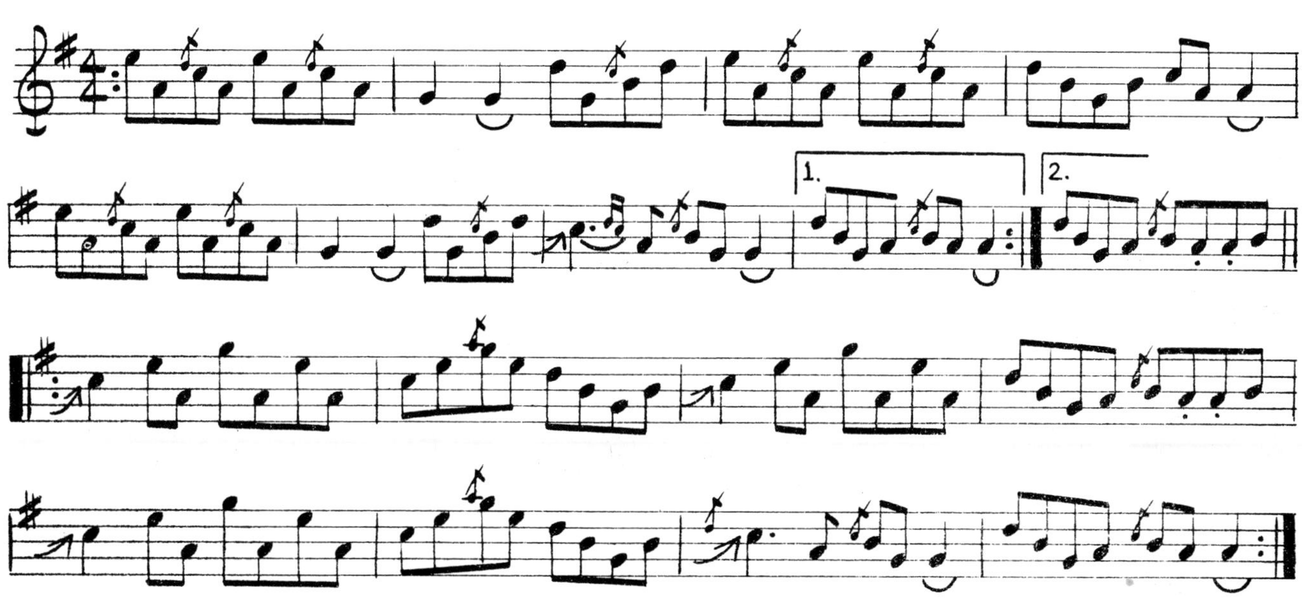

117 The Gander in the Pratie Hole

OMB 39

118 The Flogging Reel

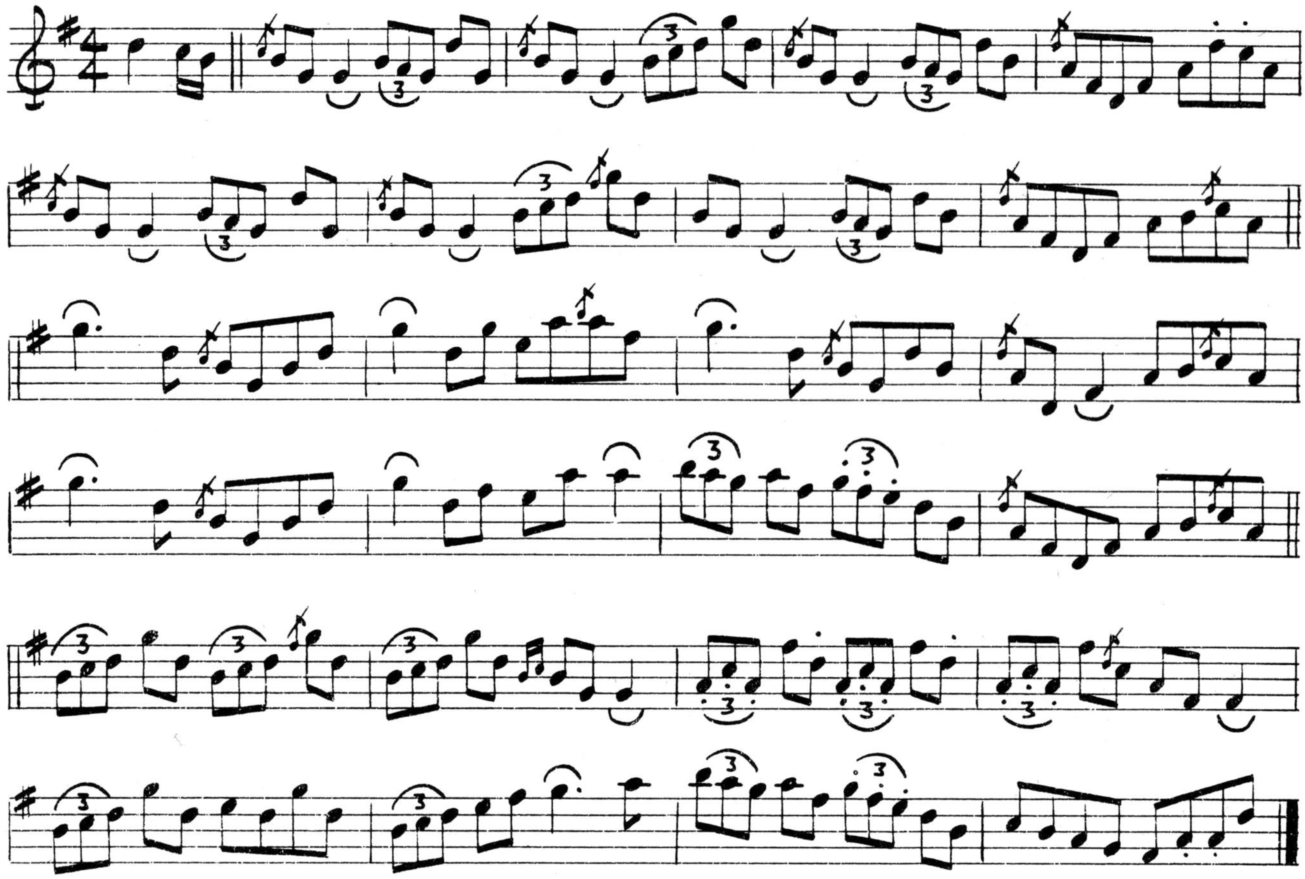

119 The Battle of Aughrim

120 Over the Moor to Maggie

121 The Sligo Maid

OMB 39

122 The Pinch of Snuff

123 Give us a Drink of Water

124 Jenny Picking Cockles

125 Brian O'Lynn

OMB 39

126 Unknown

127 Hardiman the Fiddler

128 The Trip We Took Over the Mountains

129 Follow me up to Carlow

130 The Old Man Rocking the Cradle

131 The Derry Hornpipe

OMB 39

132 The Galtee Reel

133 Ard an Bhothair

134 Tá'n Coileach ag Fógairt an Lae

135 An Buachaill Dreoite

136 An Buachaill Dreoite

137 Banish Misfortune

138 Rodney's Glory

OMB 39

139 The Gold Ring

140 The Cameronian

OMB 39

141 The Galbally Farmer

142 The Boyne Hunt

143 Ask my Father

144 Jenny's Welcome to Charlie

145 The Hurler's March

146 Fling No. 1

147 The Yellow Wattle

148 Banish Misfortune

149 Fling No. 2

150 Nóra Críona

151 Nóra Críona

152 Nóra Críona

The Range and Fingering of the Chanter

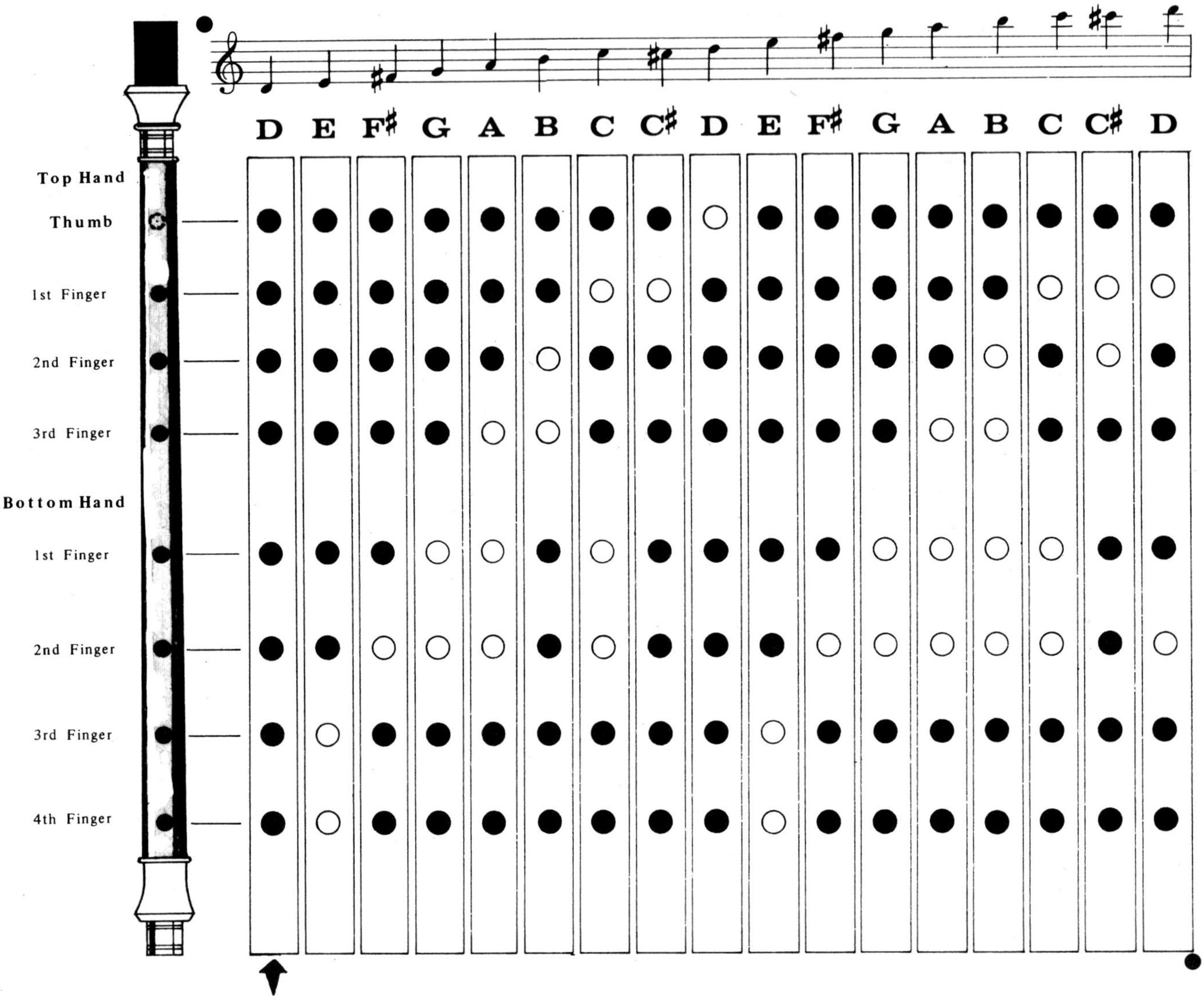

THE RANGE AND FINGERING OF THE CHANTER

Closed vents are indicated by ●, open vents by ○. The chanter is normally rested on a soft leather strap, called a popping strap, worn above the knee. This ensures that the chanter is perfectly airtight when all vents are closed thus enabling the second octave to be sounded and staccato fingering to be used. The bottom or bell note is the only one for which the chanter *must* be lifted off the popping strap. C' is the highest note normally used in Irish music and to make this note readily obtainable without having to resort to cross-fingering of harmonics, a key, which is operated by the thumb of the lower hand, is usually fitted to the chanter. Chanters have been made in pitches from B♭ to E♭, but in all instances the bell note is D.

The Tuning of the Regulators

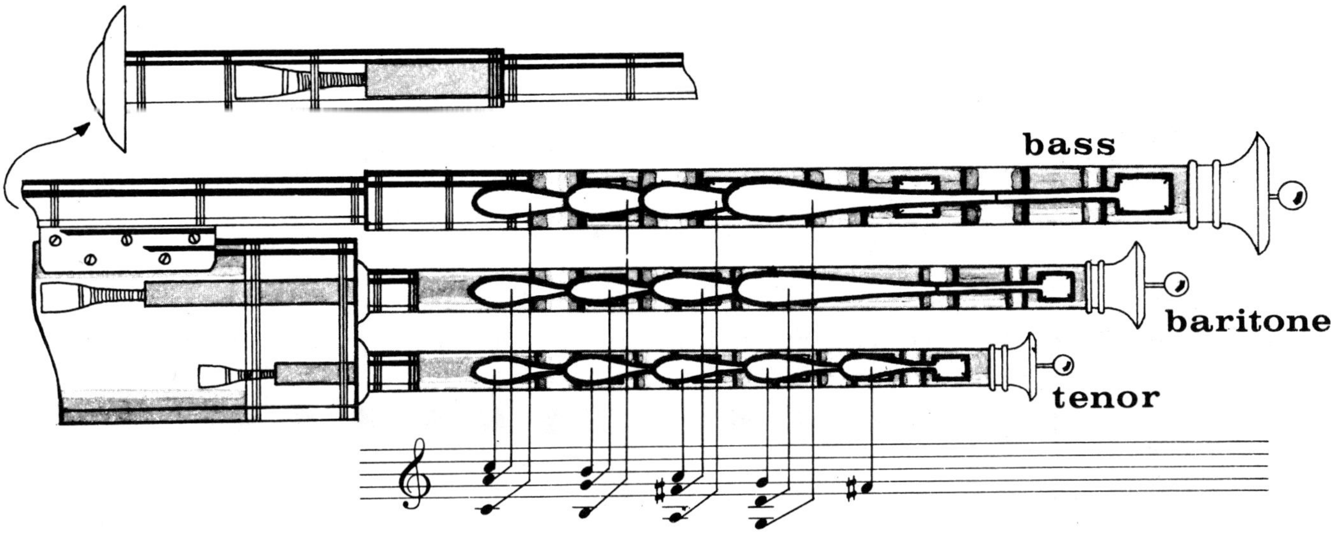

The Tuning of the Drones

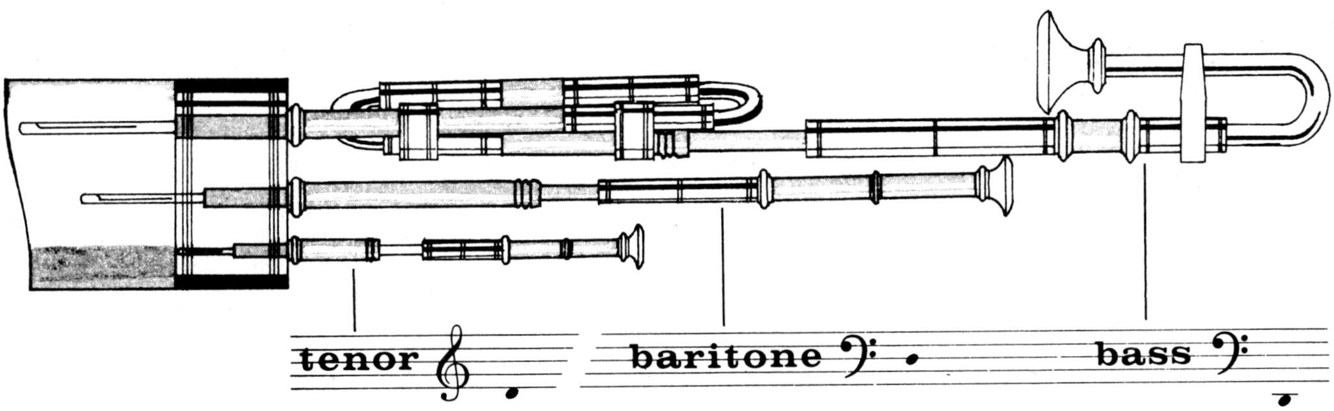

OMB 39

Ornamentation for Pipes and other Instruments

The triplet of grace notes is called a roll (example A above). If associated with a dotted crotchet this ornament is called a long roll (example B above). The long roll might be written as a crotchet followed by two semi-quavers, the first cut with a grace note above it in pitch, the second with a grace note below it in pitch. The form of ornamentation shown for the lower 'D' and 'E' on the pipes (example at C above) is known as a cran and is peculiar to this instrument.

These two tables are reproduced from Breandán Breathnach's Ceol Rince na hÉireann with kind permission of the Minister for Education.

OMB 39

Discography

The following list of the commercial recordings of Willie Clancy is, as far as I can establish, complete as at 31 July 1993. The performances are solo unless otherwise stated, and 'pipes' of course means 'uilleann pipes'. Reissues have the same titles as their original issues unless otherwise stated. Possibly some privately made recordings will be released commercially in the future and certainly more reissues will appear, so the list will continue to grow. Corrections and additions would be very welcome, and should be forwarded to me at the Irish Traditional Music Archive, 63 Merrion Square, Dublin 2. (tel. 01-661 9699, fax 01-668 6260). All help will be acknowledged.

1956

IRISH JIGS, REELS AND HORNPIPES (pipes on tracks A2-3, B1, B3, B6; pipes in duet with Michael Gorman, Sligo, fiddle, on A4-7, B4-5), Folkways FW 6819, New York (10" LP)
- A6, B4 reissued c. 1958 on IRISH PIPE AND FIDDLE TUNES, Topic TOP 89, London (EP, see next entry)
- A6 reissued 1965 on THE FOLK BOX, Elektra BOX, New York (LPs)*
- Reissued 1962 Folkways FP 6819, New York (LP)
- Duplicated on order from c. 1990 by Smithsonian Folkways Records, Washington D.C., as no 06819 (cassette)*

Information from Joe Crane, Newcastle upon Tyne

c. 1958

IRISH PIPE AND FIDDLE TUNES (pipes on A1, B2; pipes in duet with Michael Gorman, Sligo, fiddle, on A3, B3 - reissued tracks from previous entry), Topic TOP 89, London (EP)
- B2 reissued c. 1967 on FROM ERIN'S GREEN SHORE, Topic TPS 168, London (LP)

1960

As Liam Clancy (pipes), air: 'Na Connerys', Gael-Linn CE 12, Dublin (78)
- Reissued on NA CEIRNÍNÍ 78 (1957-1960), Gael-Linn CEF 075, Dublin (LP)

As Liam Clancy (pipes), reels: 'An tSean-Sceach', 'Ríl Mhichíl Uí Cheithearnaigh' [The Old Bush, Michael Carney's Reel], Gael-Linn CE 14 Dublin (78)

As Liam Clancy (pipes), hornpipes: 'Má Luirc', 'Ríl [sic] Mhichíl Uí Ghallchobhair' [The Plains of Boyle, Michael Gallagher's Reel], Gael-Linn CE 18 Dublin (78)
- Reissued 1978 on NA CEIRNÍNÍ 78 (1957-1960), Gael-Linn CEF 075, Dublin (LP), the second item as 'Rogha Uí Ghallchobhair' [Gallagher's Fancy]

1963

TRADITIONAL MUSIC OF IRELAND Vol. 1. THE OLDER TRADITIONS OF CONNEMARA AND CLARE (pipes on A3, A4), Folkways FW 8781, New York (LP)
- Duplicated on order from c. 1990 by Smithsonian Folkways Records, Washington D.C., as no 08781 (cassette)
- Reissued 1990 Cló Iar-Chonnachta CIC 033, Galway (cassette)

TRADITIONAL MUSIC OF IRELAND Vol. 2. SONGS AND DANCES FROM DOWN, KERRY AND CLARE (pipes on B1-3, B5; whistle B6-7), Folkways FW 8782, New York (LP)
- Duplicated on order from c. 1990 by Smithsonian Folkways Records, Washington D.C., as no 08782 (cassette)
- Reissued 1971 as TRADITIONAL MUSIC OF IRELAND, Michael Marc Ltd WG-971-1 / SS 22789-01, USA (LP)
- Reissued 1990 Cló Iar-Chonnachta CIC 034, Galway (cassette)

1967

THE MINSTREL FROM CLARE (pipes on A1, A3, A7, B2, B5, B7; whistle on A2, A5, B1, B4; singing in English on A4, A6, B3, B6) Topic 12T 175, London (LP, cassette)
- Reissued 1989 Ossian OSS-23, Cork (cassette)

1968
SEODA CEOIL Vol. 1 (pipes on tracks A1-4, B8-9; whistle on B6-7), Gael-Linn, CEF 018, Dublin (reel-to-reel, LP)

1969
THE BREEZE FROM ERIN. IRISH FOLK MUSIC ON WIND INSTRUMENTS (pipes on A1, B7; whistle on B1), Topic 12T 184, London (LP, cassette)
- Reissued 1989 Ossian OSS-26, Cork (cassette)

1971
THE DRONES AND CHANTERS (pipes on B9-12), Claddagh CC 11, Dublin (LP, cassette)
- Reissued 1993 Claddagh CC 11 CD (CD)

1977
MO CHEOL THÚ (pipes on B4), Gael-Linn CEF 064, Dublin (LP, cassette)

1978
THE WEST WIND (pipes on A4, A6-7, B1, B3, B6; pipes in duet with Bobby Casey, Clare, fiddle on A1, A5, A8, B8; whistle on B7), Folktracks FSA-30-173, Devon (cassette)

1980
THE PIPERING OF WILLIE CLANCY Vol. 1 (pipes on A1-9, B1, B3-9; whistle on B2), Claddagh CC 32, Dublin (LP, cassette)
- Reissued 1993 Claddagh CC 32 CD (CD)

1981
OUR MUSICAL HERITAGE (whistle on disc 3, A10, B1), RTÉ / Fundúireacht an Riadaigh FR 001-3, Dublin (LP)

1983
THE PIPERING OF WILLIE CLANCY Vol. 2 (pipes on A1-2, A4-12, B1, B3-10, B12-13; whistle on A3, B11; story on B2), Claddagh CC 39, Dublin (LP, cassette)
- Reissued 1993 Claddagh CC 39 CD (CD)

1985
A CLARE SESSION WITH WILLIE CLANCY AND FRIENDS (pipes, in session with various musicians), Skylark SK 1003, Rhode Island (cassette)

1987
CIARÁN MAC MATHÚNA INTRODUCES MUSIC FROM CLARE & KERRY (whistle in duet with Paddy Killoran, Sligo, fiddle, on A8), RTE MC 102, Dublin (cassette)

Willie Clancy (on right) concert flute player with the Tulla Céilí Band, 1946
(Photo by courtesy of Harry Hughes)

Bibliography of major articles relating to Willie Clancy

1965

Ceol II ii 48
Letter from Willie Clancy enquiring about 'Pieces'.

Ceol II ii 70 'The Man and His Music'
Transcriptions and commentary.

1972

Ceol IV i 22 'The Humours of Glin; The Piece Way'
Transcription and commentary.

1973

Dal gCais No. 1 111
Interview with Muiris Ó Rochain and Harry Hughes

Treoir 5 2
p3 'A Last Farewell' Obituary and account of funeral.
p6 'Willie Clancy - A Beloved Genius' by Martin Talty

1974

Dal gCais No. 2
p74 'The Piper - in praise of Willie Clancy'
Poem by Brian V. Mooney.
p77 'Willie Clancy - His Life and His Music
by Seamus Mac Mathúna.
p83 'Scoil Eigse Willie Clancy' review by Martin Talty

1977

Dal gCais No. 3
p72 'Junior Crehan Remembers'
Extensive biographical article based on interview with Junior (Martin) Crehan. Many references to Willie Clancy.
p79 'Lament for Willie Clancy'. Song by Junior Crehan.
p109 'Origins and Influence in the Piping of Willie Clancy'
Article by Jackie Small.
p100 'The Dance Music of Willie Clancy'. Review by Roly Brown

1988

Dal gCais No. 9 83
'Willie Clancy, His Life and Music' by Pat Mitchell

Acknowledgements

Hereunder is a list of the immediate sources from which I received material. Where appropriate, the original source is also listed in brackets. The figures in brackets indicate the year of the recording. I would like to express my thanks to all those who freely made recordings available to me.

Gael-Linn	1 - 4 from records no. CEF 14 & 18. Copyright Gael-Linn (1957)
Brian Gallahar	5 ('64), 81 - 82, 127, 134 ('68)
Breandan Breathnach (Seán Reid)	6 - 10, 13 - 22, 46 and 143 ('58) 122 ('60)
Breandan Breathnach	11 ('58), 42 - 45 ('62), 58 ('58), 59, 62, 64, 103 ('66), 60, 63, 65 ('49), 84 - 87, 89 ('61), 128 ('66)
Breandan Breathnach (An Roinn Oideachais)	12 ('66), 47 - 57 ('71), 66 - 79 ('65) 125, 126 ('66).
Breandan Breathnach (Martin Talty)	23 - 31 ('65).
Pat Mitchell	32 - 41 ('67), 117, 118, 124, 129 ('68).
Na Piobairi Uilleann	80, 83 ('68), 123 ('71), 132, 133, 135 - 142, 144 - 152 ('72).
Mrs. Rita Weill Byxbe	88, 90 - 95, 130 ('64)
Wilbert Garvin	96 - 99, 131 ('65).
Dr. Ivor Browne	61, 100 - 102, 104 - 116 ('58).
Tom Munnelly	119 - 121 ('70).

Pat Mitchell

Index

OMB 39

OMB 39

Participant (Flute) at the Willie Clancy Summer School
Photo: Liam McNulty, NPU